Love's
Three Days

A. Louis Miller

Olive Press
צהר זית

Messianic & Christian Publisher

Love's

Three Days

A. Louis Miller

Love's Three Days

Copyright © 2012 by A. Louis Miller

Cover photo by the author
Cover and interior design by Cheryl Zehr, Olive Press
Image, p. 27 copyright © 2012 shutterstock.com, used by permission.
The Damascus Gate in a 1887 print, p. 37, public domain, copyright
      expired. from Wikimedia Commons, wikimedia.org
All other drawings copyright © 2012 by
Artist, Karen Van Lieu,   *Karen A. Van Lieu*
kavanlieu@gmail.com   *Turin, NY 13473*

All Scriptures with references are taken from the New King James Version. Copyright © 1982 by Thomas Nelson, Inc. All rights reserved. Scriptures within conversations and the narrative are very close, but not exact quotes.

Published by

Olive Press
Messianic and Christian Publisher
www.olivepresspublisher.org
olivepressbooks@gmail.com

OlivePress
צהר זית

Messianic & Christian Publisher

Our prayer at Olive Press is that we may help make the Word of Adonai fully known, that it spread rapidly and be glorified everywhere. We hope our books help open people's eyes so they will turn from darkness to Light and from the power of the adversary to God and to trust in ישוע Yeshua (Jesus). (From II Thess. 3:1; Col. 1:25; Acts 26:18,15 NRSV *New Revised Standard Version* and CJB *Complete Jewish Bible*) May this book in particular cause hearts to fall more in love with our Savior.

ISBN **978-0-9790873-7-0**
1. Resurrection Day (Easter) 2. Biblical Studies - Jesus
3. Poetry : Inspirational & Religious

Dedication

With thanksgiving I dedicate this book first, to GOD who gave to us HIS Son, and gave me the inspiration for this book. May it accomplish all that He has purposed when the inspiration was given. Second, to Yeshua (Jesus), without whose life, death and resurrection, our salvation would not be possible and in whose honor this book is written.

Explanation of the Cover Photo

This photo was designed specifically to give a message in a little story sort of way. I placed the crown of thorns reverently on a Jewish Tallit—similar to the one our Jewish Messiah would have worn. I found it very interesting that the thorns come in the form of little crosses. So, I added a little cross-shaped thorn to the center of the crown. Then, I draped three strings of the Tzitzit over the right side of the thorn crossbar to represent the Love of Yeshua for His Jewish brothers for whom He died, and three strands under the left side to represent His love for the Gentiles for whom He also died.

Acknowledgements

From the depths of my heart I want to thank my wife, Linda, and our children, Sara and Joshua, for all their love and encouragement for creating this book, and Pamela for her help getting the book ready for the publisher. I'm also grateful to everyone who has given their support.

Table of Contents

Love's First Day

1

The Tears

As the near lifeless body of Miriam's (Mary's) son hung limply on the crucifixion stake, the tears she had suppressed the last thirty-three years now flowed freely from her motherly eyes.

> The tears
> She knew deep in her heart
> Would someday come,
> Now came
> With no comfort.

The tears did not come the day she was overshadowed by the Holy Spirit of God and conceived in her womb the Son of God, the child who would grow to impact every generation of mankind thereafter.

Although on the brink, the tears still did not come when her condition was, for a short while, gravely misunderstood by Yosef (Joseph), her espoused.

The tears did not come in the cold stable on the night she gave birth to the child of promise.

Nor did they come the night Yosef (Joseph) was awakened from sleep and told by the angel to flee with the child to Egypt.

Were they tears of sorrow?
Sorrow for the imminent death
Of her first born son?

Were they tears of joy?
She knew that this man
Hanging there
Was bringing salvation
To a lost and dying world.

For whatever the reason,
The long awaited tears
Finally came.

They came in a flood
As the body of her son, Yeshua (Jesus),
Hung there, barely recognizable
To her and the friends with her
At the foot of the stake;

As He hung there bleeding from the
more than three hundred fifty flesh wounds
administered by the scourging soldier;

As He hung there
Suspended
By three huge, rough nails.

2
His Hands

His hands:
The gentle hands of the man
That had picked up
 little children,
Blessing them,
Telling His followers to live
 as each of them
With unquestioning faith.

Those same healing hands
That had made mud
To restore sight to a blind man.

The life-giving hands
That had raised the widow's son
From his funeral pile,
And had raised Jairus' dead daughter.

These same gentle, loving hands
Also had a strong and forceful side.

The strong hands
That had overturned the tables
Of the money-changers
In the Temple
Erected to His Father.

The hands that a day earlier had broken bread with His twelve disciples as an example to them and us of how to remember Him.

Afterwards these hands washed the feet of the twelve as an act of servanthood.

The betrayed hands
That had dipped the bread
With His betrayer,
Judas Iscariot.

The hands of Yeshua,
God's only begotten Son,
Had now been stopped;
Nailed to the rough wooden stake,
His reward for the good He had done.

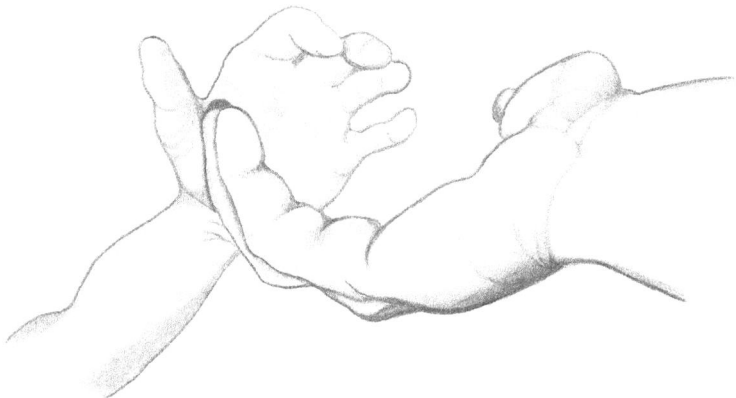

3
His Feet

His feet:
The same feet
That had walked
   the brown soil
Of His earthly
   home, Israel.

The feet that wore the sandals
John the Baptist felt unworthy
To unlatch.

The tanned, dusty feet
The prostitute had washed
With her tears
And dried with her hair.
The feet she ceased not to kiss
When she found forgiveness for her sins.

The same feet that had walked
On the Sea of Galilee.

These feet
That had been made to walk
The way of suffering
To Golgotha's Hill,
Were now nailed
One over the other to the stake.
Why?
Because
He was the Son of God.

4

His Pain

As Yeshua hung there,
His pain was His only comfort.
The pain of the gouging nails.
The humiliating pain
Of the two inch thorns,
Mockingly made into a crude crown,
And beaten into His head
To proclaim Him Israel's king.

The agonizing pain
Of His ripped flesh,
Mingled with slivers from the stake
He was forced to carry.

Salty,
Stinging
Drops of sweat
That flowed through the open cuts
Added their part to His pain.

He still felt the pain
Of the blows to His face and
From the plucking of His beard.

All of His pain was multiplied by the
sheer exhaustion of the previous night and
earlier part of that day.

The pain He was feeling was
     unimaginable.
Yet, amidst the physical pain,
Yeshua felt an even more intense pain.
The pain of rejection and
Ridicule, and the mocking hatred
Of some of His own people.
Due to their spiritual blindness

He felt the deep-rooted pain everyone
on that hill that day would feel. He labored
under the pain felt by His followers who were
scattered hours before. He felt all the pain the
children of Abraham, Isaac and Jacob would
feel for two thousand years to come. Yeshua
was feeling all of that pain, hanging there.
     The intensity of the pain brought with
it a small measure of comfort as Yeshua hung
there. Yet, it paled in comparison to what was
still to come.

     As the sky darkened that afternoon,
the spectators to Yeshua's crucifixion feared
rain. But what were threatening clouds to the
gathered crowd, was to be for Yeshua the
reason He had come to earth. As the night-
black clouds gathered over the hill called "The
Skull" and over Jerusalem, God began the
painful process of laying on His Son the sins
of every human being that would ever live.
     From Adam to Noah,
     From Noah on down to Abraham.

From Abraham down through all the
generations of his descendants, and all who
were born out of the Abrahamic bloodline,
Up to that afternoon.
From that day on,
And on down through the years
To the end of this current age.
Every ugly, black, God-hated sin
Would be put upon Him that ever-
darkening afternoon.
With the weight and pain of all that sin,
Also came a promise.
Death.
"For the wages of sin is death."
Yet, before death could come,
Yeshua would experience even greater
pain.

With the sins of all mankind having been
laid on His sinless life, Yeshua hung limp on
the stake. Breathing was getting increasingly
harder with each passing minute. His perfect
life, now marred, was slowly slipping away
from His earthly body. In this pathetic state,
He was about to experience an unexplainable
pain—the pain of separation from God that
would be felt by billions of souls.
He would feel the pain of those souls
separated from the God who loves them,
because they would choose the pleasures of
sin over God's faithful love. Yeshua felt that
pain billions of times over. It was by far more
painful than all of the physical pain His body
now felt.

It was our pain.
He bore it for all of
      humanity.
He bore our sins.
He bore our pain.
What love!

As Yeshua hung there close to death, He was aware of an even more painful experience still to come. A pain possibly felt one other time since the creation of the earth. Had God, the greatest love in the universe, felt the pain His Son was about to know? Had God's great heart been broken when the first man, Adam, chose to disobey Him, and thus separated the creature from the Creator?

5

His Broken Heart

As the massing clouds reached their darkest, and the life-sustaining sun was now blacked out, it happened. For the second time since eternity past, God's heart would be broken. God would now have to treat His Holy Son the same as fallen man. He would turn His face away from His Son.

He would have to.

He could not now look upon Him with all of our sins on Him.

The moment God turned away from Him, Yeshua felt the most unbearable of all pain. A pain no human could ever really know while still in the body.

The pain of being separated from God.
The pain would break His heart of love.
His broken heart
Would cause His perfect life to cease.
He would die there on the crucifixion
stake,
Bearing in his body the sins of all
humanity,
So we wouldn't have to know
The separation from God
That He now knew.

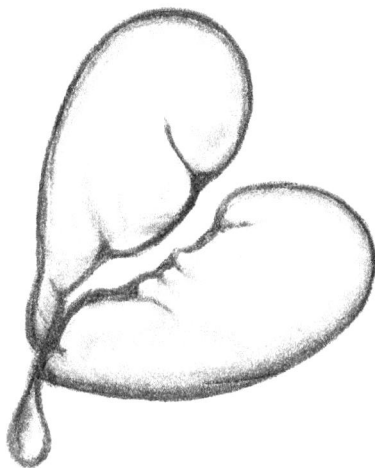

As Yeshua hung there in total agony, minutes from death, He heard laughter. He heard the scornful laughter of some in the crowd still gathered there. He anguished over the uncaring laughter of the Roman soldiers as they cast lots for His only earthly possessions.

> The clothing stripped from His body.
> There was also the laughter that only
> He could hear.
> The mocking, sneering laughter of the
> host of hell.
> A hideous laughter proclaiming a soon
> to be,
> "Victory over the helpless Son of the
> Most High God."

6

It Is Finished

"Soon."

"Soon the imposter will be ours," snarled one of the two foul creatures standing unseen at the base of the stake. A grotesque laughter echoed through the unseen realm.

"Where is Your God now, imposter?" The other sneered, as a sulphurous smelling drool oozed from its twisted mouth. The unseen realm reeked with this suffocating odor. The smell of death and hell.

"Will this God You so foolishly served come to Your rescue?" one of them growled. "No, He will leave You to us even as He has left all the rest of pathetic mankind to us, to do with as we please."

Aware of the presence of the two hideous, reeking creatures, Yeshua hung, submitted to the weight of the sin now upon Him. He had seen the evil pair, Satan's two strongest demons, shackles in hand, waiting. Waiting for the moment of His death. Waiting to shackle Him and lead Him triumphantly back with them to the abode of the dead. Sensing that their wait was almost over, the two excited demons began to laugh more hideously than ever. The black air filled with the grotesque laughter of the unnumbered host of hell. The excitement and anticipation

24

of centuries of waiting was almost over. "Our master will soon own the rights to all of creation," the commander of all of hell's forces said.

"Soon," answered his subordinate excitedly. "Soon!" He followed with a long, grotesque, stench fuming laugh.

Unnoticed at first by the two occupied demons, the body of Yeshua convulsed—an almost futile effort to raise Himself up, as if gasping for a breath. As the last act of His earthly life, Yeshua would speak three final words—three words that would reverberate through the corridors of time, bringing hope to many who would come to trust in Him. The sound of the three words so shocked the devilish sentries of the crucifixion stake, that they were caught totally off guard.

> With His last ounce of strength,
> Yeshua let out a triumphant,
> "IT IS FINISHED."
> His body then slumped to Its death.
> His life ended.

The two demons, who by now had regained their composure, joyfully prepared to shackle their newest "Fool," as they so enjoyed calling all who die. As they readied their shackles, horror seized them. Instead of Yeshua's spirit falling submissively to them, to their surprise, It rose into the sun-denied air over Calvary. Just as quickly, the spirit of Yeshua descended into the earth between the two stunned creatures with such force, the earth quaked. A split occurred in the earth that traveled directly across the hole that the crucifixion stake had been placed in. The stunned pair left behind, immediately followed their prey in hot pursuit.

At the same instant that Yeshua's spirit split the earth, souls of some of the dead, buried in Jerusalem, rose and appeared to some of the residents there. Were they a First Fruit Offering by Yeshua to His Father?

The pursuing duo was brought to an immediate halt.

Stunned by a voice so fearful, they could only huddle together and tremble. And these were Satan's two strongest warriors.

7
The Voice

The voice:

The voice that had commanded the legion of demons out of a man and into a herd of swine.

The same voice that said, "Let him who is without sin cast the first stone" to the crowd that had brought the woman caught in the act of adultery. And a few minutes later said to the woman, "Woman, where are thine accusers?" And, "I also do not accuse you. Go and sin no more."

The powerful voice that called Lazarus from death four days after he had died.

That same voice,

Now more fearful,

With more power,

Thundered through the bowels of the earth.

That voice now shook the very foundations of Sheol and Hades, the abode of the dead.

The victorious voice of Yeshua, which a moment ago was barely able to speak,

Now thundered.

Repeating His final Words on the stake,

He spoke with a commanding confidence,

"IT IS FINISHED."

It was like music to the hearing of those who were with the righteous Abraham, while striking terror on the other side of the great divide.

Victorious and in unparalleled brilliance, Yeshua stood at the edge of a great divide separating hell from what has been called The Bosom of Abraham, somewhere in the center regions of the earth. The light of His countenance engulfed all of the faithful there with Abraham, the father of the Jewish race, while the hell side remained in its dark, sulphurous state. In the light was an incomprehensible peace, and the expectation of an exodus more glorious than the first exodus of Israel's children.

An exodus to a better place.
A place of everlasting life
Where sickness and death
Are not to be found.
A home
Where love rules
And peace abounds.
The place Yeshua taught about many
        times during His earthly ministry.
Heaven
His Heavenly Father's kingdom

The hell side was astir with frantic confusion in both the host of hell and their captives.

The air on the newly bright side now had a fragrance of indescribable sweetness to it. A fragrance of life never experienced before by the souls waiting there. A cool, gentle breeze suddenly blew through that portion of the inner earth for the first time. The breeze carried the sweet fragrance to the furthest reaches of Abraham's Bosom, bringing renewed life to the soon-to-be redeemed and released throng of jubilant souls.

The other side of the great chasm sat in fearful wonder at the spectacle before their eyes. From his dark, death-reeking chamber, Satan, vehemently cursing and screaming, denies the scene. This side was dark and extremely hot, with a stench of ten thousand sun-baked garbage dumps. A sulphuric mist hung heavily in the air throughout the cavernous waste. In addition, there were hundreds of smells one could not even imagine. Demons and imps ran excitedly back and forth through the dark dungeon, sometimes running into each other in their confusion. All of them screaming, cursing, crying, and afraid, yet somehow maintaining organization, and loyalty to their cruel taskmaster. The souls of the dead there hearing the tormenting sound could only wonder, terrified, what the commotion was all about.

Still in darkness
Still in chains
Bound forever for a life of unbelief

    Satan, in his disgust, muttered to nothing and no one in particular, "Where are my two failures? Why I ever promoted them to their positions I'll never understand."
    If the whereabouts of the two demons had been known, they would have been discovered in a damp cave far from the ensuing confrontation.

8
The Burial

Warm drops of the remaining life-giving blood of Yeshua's now lifeless body, now slumped on the now tilting execution stake, were brought forth by a Roman soldier's spear. The blood, mixed with water, signaled the finality of death. The thrust of the spear into Yeshua's side was the only pain He did not feel that dark afternoon.

The sudden darkness had chased away most of the crowd gathered on Golgotha's hill. They were saying that they had to go and make ready the Passover. Was the darkness of their sins too much to confront that stark moment? Would they ever confront their sinfulness after that unforgettable day?

Knowing that Hebrew law stated that dead bodies had to be taken down from the stakes and buried before sundown on the eve of Passover, a secret follower of Yeshua, named Nicodemus, and a man from Arimathea, called Yosef (Joseph), asked for permission to take the body. Permission granted, they removed Yeshua's lifeless form from the stake, deciding to carry it to a tomb nearby for a quick burial. "After the Passover, we will properly prepare Him for entombment," Nicodemus told his new friend.

As Nicodemus and Yosef began wrapping the body on the hilltop before transporting it—at that same moment, unnoticed to them, some of the shed blood of Yeshua had found its way into the crack that ran through the hill, the result of the earthquake earlier. It ran from corner to corner across the hole dug for the placement of the execution stake. It was into that crack some of Yeshua's precious blood flowed. As the men finished wrapping the body in troubled silence, many thoughts tormented them concerning this innocent man's cruel crucifixion.

As they began carrying the lifeless body of Yeshua, His spirit was appearing to Abraham in the bowels of the earth. Abraham and those with him were in awe at the sight of the radiant image that stood before them with arms outstretched.

"I Am He whom you have been waiting for," Yeshua spoke. Immediately, almost as if they had been rehearsing, the multitude of souls bowed in unison before Him as their shouts of joyous celebration rose to greet Him. The shouts sent great fear through the halls and caverns of the abode of the unrighteous dead. "I have come to take you to my Father," Yeshua started again. "But first I have a work to finish. I will return to you shortly." As suddenly as He had appeared to them, He was gone. Not one soul in the Bosom of Abraham questioned what had just happened. They just rejoiced the more, with joy unspeakable and full of glory. The Messiah had come.

As Nicodemus and Yosef carried away their hope, Nicodemus first began to talk. "It just does not seem like the Master any more. It feels like just another dead body."

"Be comforted, my friend," said Yosef. "Think about the many wonderful things He spoke of, and the miracles He performed while He was alive."

"I know," answered the weary Pharisee. "I remember a conversation I had with Him a couple of years ago." He paused, then went on. "I told Him that I knew He was a teacher that had come from God. He said to me, 'Most assuredly, unless a man is born again, he cannot see the Kingdom of God.' I was confused as to how to be born again, and He said, 'Unless one is born of water and of the Spirit, he cannot enter the Kingdom of God. That which is born of the flesh is flesh, and that which is born of the Spirit is Spirit.' Then He went on to say, 'The wind blows where it wishes, and you hear the sound of it, but you cannot tell where it comes from or where it goes. So is everyone who is born of the Spirit.'"

Yosef answered, "Did you fully understand His meaning?"

"I asked Him how this thing could be," said Nicodemus. "He answered me and said, 'Are you the teacher of Israel, and do not know these things?' I was speechless. So He said to me, 'Truly we speak what we know and testify what we have seen, and you do not receive our witness. If I have told you earthly things and you do not believe, how will you believe if I tell you Heavenly things? No one has ascended to Heaven but He who came down from Heaven, that is, the Son of Man, who is in Heaven. And as Moses lifted up the serpent in the wilderness, even so must the Son of Man be lifted up, that whoever believes in Him should not perish but have everlasting life.'" With that, Nicodemus was overtaken by a thought that stopped him cold.

"What is the matter, my friend?" Yosef asked in a voice showing great concern.

"What He said to me that night," Nicodemus answered. "'Even so must the Son of Man be lifted up.' He was lifted up, on the crucifixion stake, and killed, just like He said He had to be. Now all who believe can be with Him in His Father's Kingdom."

Yosef sensing his excitement, said, "I remember hearing Him myself once say, 'As Jonah was in the belly of the whale three days and three nights, so must the Son of Man be three days and three nights in the belly of the earth.'" A peace beyond any of the words either man could speak, or beyond any of their human understanding had just now overcome them both. The glorious thought that in three days the dead body they carried would be alive again was more than they could bear. Filled with joy and much peace, the body they carried now seemed weightless to them.

"Do you believe, Nicodemus?" His friend asked.

"That this Yeshua is truly the Son of God, and Israel's Messiah? Yes, my friend," he answered, "I do believe."

"So also do I, " added the man from Arimathea.

A warm glow filled both men. If they could have seen, at that very minute, Yeshua, in all His Glory stood with them as the Spirit of the Living God—indwelling and filling them both. Everlasting life had been imparted to them because of their belief—everlasting life in the form of God's Holy Spirit. After a hug in the Spirit to both men from Yeshua, He was, in an instant, back to His appointed task.

As the two men left the borrowed tomb in which they laid the body of their Messiah, and the Roman soldiers rolled the stone across its entrance, a shofar could be heard in the distance, calling Israel to the feast of Passover.

Love's Second Day

9
The Victory

Across the divide from Abraham's Bosom, Hades was in a state of turmoil. Spirits of darkness were frantically going round and round, and running back and forth with no idea of what had just transpired. Fear and confusion gripped all of them as the powerful presence of Yeshua, not at all the cowering, fearful soul they were expecting, stood in their midst. Their hissing, venomous orders to Him going unheeded caused grave concern to the lieutenants in Satan's evil army. They were, up till now, used to cowering souls blindly obeying their hideous commands. This was not natural to them. Fear began to grip the once fearless, dark soldiers.

"Why does He not cower in fear before us?" Spoke one of them in a scratchy, deep-throated voice.

"He will learn," snarled another.

A third demon, a huge, black, winged creature, ended all conversation, saying,

"The master will put Him in His place. Leave Him and get about your duties." In a show of fearful obedience, the gathered horde dispersed in a flurry of flapping wings, and a cloud of sulphurous-smelling vapor.

Down a pitch black corridor, fuming mad at the failure of his two guards sent to escort his greatest prize, nervously came the great deceiver. "How dare He think He has won?" He said aloud to himself. "I shall have the last and only laugh at this poor excuse of a Savior for mankind. He could not remain alive in the world of His own making. Now He's dead. He's in my domain. He cannot leave, ever. He's MINE." The destroyer of souls boasted in the unhearing darkness.

As he came to the place where Yeshua now waited, he let out the most blood curdling laugh. Every soul and spirit in Hades shuddered at the laugh, save one. Upon seeing his arch enemy not move so much as an eyelash, fear gripped the master of fear. He thought, "Something does not seem right here," but kept his composure, as well as a leader can who has just realized there has been a breach in his power. After all, he had to encourage his horde that he was still in charge here.

Smiling a sly grin, Satan tried to be as evilly polite as he could be. Standing some fifty paces from Yeshua, his faithful fallen army behind him, he spoke first. "Welcome to your new home." He paused for emphasis. "Get used to your surroundings. You are going to be here for a while," he added with more vile laughter.

Suddenly his countenance changed from a hideous kindness to a dark evil anger. "Fool," he said, "you have lost. This is my finest victory. I have killed the so-called Son of God, the supposed Savior of the world. You can never escape here now. YOU ARE MINE!"

A chorus of sulphuric cheers erupted in Hades at Satan's futile boast. The scene was a show of demons jumping and dancing, and shouting all manner of foul, vulgar words at the still imposing, and yet unmoving presence of God's only begotten Son.

With a voice that not only commanded obedience, but also caused it to be, Yeshua shouted, "SILENCE!" Instantly Hades was as quiet as the space and time prior to the creation. Some demons actually fainted, to the disgust of their leader. Some cowered in fear, hiding behind others who were trying to hide themselves. Still others, Satan included, put on a facade of fearlessness. "I have come for what is mine," said Yeshua.

Trying to look like the leader he hoped he still was, Satan responded, "What is rightfully yours is the cell at the far side of the great room. Now get there!" He stamped his foot for added impact. Sensing a loss of control, but not showing it, he stood there gloating in his response.

"I have come to proclaim liberty to the captive." Yeshua continued, not paying any attention to the rambling of His adversary. "Now I command you, Satan, and your horde, to be in silence."

Not another sound was heard for the span of about thirty earth minutes save the sweet, tender voice of the Son of God.

Yeshua began to speak to the tormented souls in Hades with compassion and conviction, "My Father created the heavens and the earth. Seeing the need for a recipient for His great love, He made man from the dust of the earth. My Father made man in His image, and seeing that man needed companionship, He made from the man's rib a woman. They were made for each other, and also to have fellowship with God.

"The man and woman had everything my Father had created at their disposal. They were to keep the garden, in which my Father had placed them, fruitful, and, were to multiply their seed upon the earth. All of you here and across the great gulf behind me are the seed of the first man and woman.

"One day back in the garden, Satan, an angel fallen from the service of my Father, tempted the woman to disobey the requirements of my Father, telling her it was okay to eat the fruit of the tree my Father had strictly forbidden them to eat. The woman succumbed to his beguiling words and did eat, and persuaded also the man to do likewise. That opened the door for sin to enter into my Father's created earth.

"Sin broke the fellowship mankind once had with my Father. Since that time, mankind has been in need of a savior to redeem them and bring them back to God.

"My Father promised the man and woman that He would send them a Redeemer. Since that time, some of mankind has tried to live in obedience to the commands set forth by my Father and handed down from generation to generation. They are those across the great dividing gulf. They are redeemed already because of their obedience and their belief. Yet I still needed to come to tell the Good News to you who have not heard or have heard wrong.

"The Good News is that God my Father has sent me to die instead of you for your transgressions against His commands. I freely gave up my place in Heaven with my Father, to take on the form of man, to be tempted as man, yet without sin. Being without sin, I was immune to human death, for the wages of sin is death.

"I freely chose to die, to give up my life for fallen man. I chose to take the sins of all of mankind on me and to forfeit my sinless life for theirs. That means all the sins of everyone here and across the gulf in Abraham's Bosom, as well as everyone still alive on the earth and everyone yet to be born for countless ages still to come. I have carried every single sin to my death. You are all forgiven if you will only believe. If you will believe you will be free to leave with me this very day."

As Yeshua finished speaking, Satan violently protested, "You are lying. You have no power here. I hold the keys to death, hell, and the grave." He ranted on, "These fools are mine. I won them fair and square."

"Be silent, Deceiver!" Yeshua responded, adding, "All who believe my report are free to come with me."

"Fools," desperately screeched Satan. "He is lying. You are mine! Stay put or else!" Satan had begun to muster some courage, and in so doing his actions encouraged some of his more fearsome soldiers to find a false courage also. As he started to move towards Yeshua, he snarled at some sobbing souls who now, in a new-found boldness began to stand and move towards where the Son of God stood. "Get back to your holes," Satan's venomous voice snarled.

"Resist," commanded Yeshua. "He has no more power over you. I have defeated him. Only believe."

"Get back here, you maggots. I own you. I am your master. You are mine!" The now frantic deceiver began yelling, sensing he was losing control. As more souls saw the battle of words coming to a head, they rose to join the first wave of new believers.

Echoes of "Fools," "Come back," "He's lying," "He can't take you out of here" rose from the souls that would not have any of what Yeshua had said. The more panic stricken Satan became, the more souls rose to join the ever growing crowd gathered around Yeshua.

What happened next stunned every soul and spirit in both sides of the great divided gulf. In an instant, before Yeshua's adversary knew what hit him, He had walked up to the deceiver, and in front of all eyes, reached out His nail pierced right hand, and stripped Satan of all of his authority. He snatched the keys to death, hell, and the grave from around Satan's neck. Now no longer would death's sting be there when a believer died, for now they would know that to die was to be present with the Lord.

Without his authority and the keys, Satan was powerless to stand in the presence of his conqueror. Cowering away, defeated, he was also powerless to prevent another exodus.

This great exodus of newly redeemed souls.

However, though a vast multitude of souls chose to follow Yeshua out of their place of torment, many remained deceived and stayed in their torment, choosing rather to believe the lie.

As the growing crowd of souls that chose to follow Yeshua amassed at the edge of the gulf, questions arose as to how they were going to get over to the other side. As they stood there, a few of the deceived followers of Satan began to muster up enough courage to make a rear assault in hopes of striking fear in the group now growing larger by the earth minute.

Keeping a safe distance though, the horde began to yell at the escaping spirits, but their commands to get back to their places fell on deaf ears. Sensing hopelessness, the rebellious souls began to try to verbally instill doubts into the newly redeemed minds, "See, there is no way out of here." "He has deceived you." "He also is one of us." "He only got your hopes up so that we could bring you back to your true reward." And, "See, he lies just like us, so get back here, NOW!" These and many other desperate words the hellish horde spoke in hopes of finding favor in the eyes of their now humiliated, yet very angry master.

Though the barrage of lies was very hard on their ears, the souls with Yeshua knew that they had to resist with all they had—especially those furthest from Him. They found encouragement in each other and in the words that Yeshua had spoken, still resounding in their ears, and in the peace that encompassed the whole of them emanating from the Prince of Peace. A peace they did not understand. A peace they instinctively knew they would be foolish to walk away from. A true peace that all of them were feeling for the very first time.

10
The Deliverance

Gathered together with Yeshua at the edge of the dividing gulf was a large congregation of souls who were weary from centuries (or for some, days that seemed like centuries), of torment. They were glad to be leaving, yet not quite ready to rejoice, for ahead of them was a wide and very deep ravine. Many wondered how they were going to get across to real freedom. Behind them, though, were some things they had thought they would never be able to leave:

The flames, hot and tormenting.
The foul, putrid smell of sulphur and
    ever burning flesh.

The squealing, scratchy, pitiless voices of their tormentors now silenced by all that had just transpired.

Behind them were the pits, the cages, the whining, crying, and pitiful wails of souls without hope.

Comforting to their spirits were the words of Yeshua, "Behold, your deliverance has come."

Just then a rumbling was heard by all those present in the earth's core. Out of the deep darkness of the inner earth, from somewhere above them, descended, to their surprise, the image of a vertical and horizontal type of bridge that covered the expanse and the depth of the gulf before them. As Yeshua was put to death on a similar object, it now bridged the gap between them and the place of righteous Abraham, and those who lived in obedience to God's law.

> The same law that Yeshua had just fulfilled.
> Now all redemption was by grace through faith.
> Faith in the redeeming act of Yeshua, the Son of God.

As the first soul set foot on the bridge to Abraham's Bosom, a heavy load fell off of him—him, and each soul that followed. A load of torment and scorn, the wages of a life of sin carried on into death. The heaviness of separation from God now began to fall off of the slouched, once chained souls. As these weights fell off and the departing souls could once again stand upright, each in turn looked Yeshua in the eyes. As great tears fell, jubilant "Thank You's" were spoken by each departing soul. Hugs of love and appreciation were given by each man and woman exiting Hades that day. Yeshua kissed each new believer tenderly as they passed on over the bridge.

With each step towards the Bosom of Abraham the heat and the stench of their former dwelling place began to fade from the senses of the large crowd. Soon the first ones were totally out of the foul remembrances and were walking in a cool, sweet fragranced and light air. As they neared the edge of Abraham's Bosom, cheers rose up to greet them.

Standing first to greet each and everyone upon entrance into their new freedom, was the great patriarch himself, Abraham, through whom God had promised He would bring the blessing of the Savior. Hugs were the order of the day in Abraham's Bosom, as each entering soul was hugged at least ten thousand times, some even more.

> Hugs from loved ones.
> Hugs from souls just rejoicing to see
> them out of their torment.

> Cold, refreshing
> Living Water
> Awaited each soul crossing the divide.
> Sweeter water has never passed the lips
> of earth bound man.

> Cries of joy replaced cries of agony and
> torment.

Rejoicing was everywhere with each new soul stepping into freedom that day.

Never had there been recorded in earth history a day of such rejoicing as there was that day.

As the last departing soul entered Abraham's Bosom, Yeshua stood alone at the other end of the Cross Bridge—His heart of hearts filled with mixed emotion. He had done all that His Father had asked Him to do, and in that He was glad. Yet, multitudes of souls chose to reject His message even now. Tears filled His compassionate eyes as He looked one last time for a trailing soul He knew would not be coming. After these tears came an outpouring of more tears. This time for the many who would still reject Him in the ages to come. For those who would choose to believe the lie even now, still being perpetrated by His adversary in his determination to settle the score for the humiliating defeat he was just dealt.

As Yeshua turned to leave, His eye caught a pathetic lump huddled, cowering in a corner cave. His dull eyes opened and met Yeshua's gaze for a brief moment. The love and tender compassion in Yeshua's eyes towards the tormented soul beckoning him to come, was blocked from his view by the shame of his life's actions. Shame blinded his eyes to the forgiveness being offered in that final look from his friend. There would be no leaving the cave for this soul that day. The last eyes Yeshua would see down there, before turning to walk away forever, were those tortured eyes of Judas Iscariot, His betrayer.

11
The Enemy

Yeshua turned His back on Hades one last time. As He made the walk over the Cross Bridge, soul-piercing screams rose from the darkness and stench preserved for those who in the future would choose to deny Him. Horrifying cries rose from those remaining deceived souls who only now realized what had just come to pass. All that Yeshua had said to them had been true after all! Now it was too late.

In the midst of the wailing and crying an angry voice was heard shouting threats to the departing Messiah. "You haven't won anything," Satan yelled. Adding in a horrendously evil voice, "I will get you. I shall one day destroy your work. Your followers, your chosen people, I will win them over to my side. You watch and see." The empty threats went unheard by Yeshua who by this time was near enough to the other side that His ears heard only the rejoicing of the redeemed.

If Yeshua had turned around just one more time, He would have seen frantic souls running to the edge of the great divide hoping to follow Him over. Only as they reached the edge did they discover, to their horror, that the Cross Bridge was burning behind Yeshua.

No more was access out of Hades provided. In desperation, burdened with sulphurous, venomous spirits on their backs, some souls jumped over the edge in hopes of somehow making it to the other side. They soon found out how futile their efforts were. Falling for what seemed like an eternity, they were then dragged back, screaming and fighting, by Satan's horde of demons.

Satan, the former Archangel whose appearance was once as precious stones, and who once led all worship of God in Heaven, now resembled a charred piece of coal in the darkest reaches of Hell. The angel anointed to be the covering angel was now beaten, and he knew it. He now vowed to himself to destroy the humanity Yeshua had just died for.

12
The Rejoicing

Yeshua, upon greeting Abraham at
the entrance of the abode of the righteous
redeemed, was greeted with the thunder
of countless millions of voices raised in
thanksgiving and praise to Him. The praise
and thanksgiving lasted for what seemed like
many, many earth days as it reverberated
endlessly off of the walls of Abraham's
Bosom. As the inner core of souls nearest to
Yeshua began to quiet, those on the outer
edge could still be heard. As they trailed off,
the inner core would get caught up in it again
and the praise and thanksgiving would start
all over. This kept going on and on and on. It
actually lasted an entire day in earth time.

All the while Yeshua was greeting
friends new and old: Abraham, Noah,
Methuselah, and the first man, Adam, and
his wife, Eve. The twelve sons of Jacob.,
He greeted with a special acknowledgement,
Judah, from whose bloodline He had been
birthed. King David and Yeshua seemed to
talk for hours. He met families He had known
growing up. He loved them then, and He
loved them even more now. Rahab, the harlot,
hugged her great, great... (many "great's")
grandson.

Moses and Aaron and their sister, Miriam, greeted Him with great excitement. They had been in the exodus from Egypt along with Joshua and many others. "Soon you will be making another exodus," Yeshua told them. With that word more excitement filled the place as those around them heard that they would soon depart. As the word spread the excitement grew.

Yeshua greeted many, many souls that day in the Bosom of Abraham. The ones He did not get to greet there, He would meet on the way to their new home.

The last soul Yeshua greeted before He started to speak to the crowd as a whole was the last person He had had words with above. "Remember me, Lord?" the mild voice said as Yeshua came near him.

Looking at the thief that had hung on one side of Him, Yeshua answered, "Yes, my child, I remember you. Come with me."

As Yeshua turned and stood ready to speak to all who would now listen, the thief stood at His right side. The rest stood around Him as far as the eye could see.

"This day," He started, "you shall all come with me to Paradise." A jubilant cheer rose up that shook the bowels of the earth. "I have come just as the prophets have foretold," He said, pointing to Daniel and Isaiah and the rest of the men and women who throughout the ages had proclaimed His coming.

55

Yeshua continued amidst the chorus of praise, "I have taught on earth all that my Father in Heaven has instructed me to teach. I have healed the sick, delivered many from demons, and raised the dead to life again. I have left a record of my life on earth with my followers, and have given my life for the forgiveness of all sins." At these words the throng in unison knelt before Yeshua and wept tears of joy and thanksgiving. "You are all redeemed," He continued. "Free from all of your transgressions, and free to enter the Kingdom my Father has prepared for you. I have come to take you there."

A joyous celebration, unrehearsed and unlike any ever experienced before, broke out in that cavern at the words just spoken. Songs of praise were sung as Miriam, the sister of Moses, led a hundred thousand in a dance of deliverance not unlike the one she led after the children of Israel crossed over the Red Sea. A jubilant Yeshua even joined in the dance. What a glorious sight that was for the throng to behold. The Bosom of Abraham had never known such joy before.

The joy of the Lord.
The joy of redemption.

13

Paradise

After the dance, which seemed to go
on for days, Yeshua continued to address
the faithful. "Your many, long years of
waiting and anticipating are over. We shall
be departing here now." More joyous praise
erupted. Yeshua again spoke, "You shall not at
this time be joined to your earthly bodies, but
the time is coming when you shall receive new
glorified bodies. For now you shall remain as
you are, in spirit form."

After saying that, He moved through
the crowd to the furthest back edge of
Abraham's Bosom. He came to a door in
the earthen wall unnoticed by anyone until
now. When opened, it led into a well lighted
hallway.

"This is the way, come, follow me,"
He said.

With no semblance of fear, the multitude
followed Yeshua into a light that went higher
up than they had ever been. The bright
hallway appeared to ascend upward forever.
Many wondered where the outer edge of
the earth was. They would wonder, but they
would never see it.

The corridor seemed to take days to traverse when in reality it took only a few earth minutes. When Yeshua did finally stop, He could look down the corridor for miles and miles and see the joyful throng behind Him.

Songs rang out all the way down the hall of light. The joy He felt at that moment could never be put into words, but all believers shall know it one day.

"We are there!" Yeshua's great voice echoed down the long corridor, so that everyone heard it. More jubilant praise rose to fill the corridor of freedom.

Before turning to enter with His followers into Paradise, Yeshua had one last thing to say to them. Lifting His loving voice in song-like manner, He said,

"Well done, thou good and faithful servants. Enter into my rest."

With that He turned and walked into an even brighter light, the eternal light of the Paradise of God. As each soul crossed the threshold into Paradise, each was clothed in a robe of purest white, and was able to traverse time and space instantly.

What met their eyes was
A wonder far beyond the ability to
          describe.
The colors,
The scents,
The sounds,
All never before experienced by any
          soul,
These souls were now experiencing.

Many fell at the feet of Yeshua
And worshipped Him.
All learned
Upon walking through the final door
What Yeshua meant when He said,
"Enter into my rest."

As each soul passed through the door
          into Paradise,
The sorrows from their earthly lives,
The hurts,
The pains, and the bouts with sickness
Were instantly stricken from their
          memory.

Every soul there was finally at rest from
the toils and struggles that life had inflicted
upon them.

Every soul there now knew the peace of God that passes all understanding, and the great love the Father has for us all.

Every soul there greatly rejoiced in their Creator, in their Savior, and in their eternal home.

After what seemed like many earth days of rejoicing and singing and dancing before the Lord, and of children all playing at the feet of Yeshua, He told them He had to leave for a short season.

"Though redemption's sacrifice has been made, and I have led captivity captive and have taken the keys of Hell, death, and the grave from the adversary, My Father has more work for Me to do. I have taken you from the bowels of the earth, yet I must still purchase everlasting life for you and all who will follow after you." He went on, "When I return I will take you to my Father. Then this part of my work will be done."

As Yeshua turned to go back through the door into the corridor He was given a glorious send-off of praise and worship.

In His absence, angels appeared to welcome the mass of souls into Paradise, to show them around, and to minister unto them.

Love's Third Day

14

Father And Son

As Yeshua, the Son of God, entered the portal through which they had just arrived, an unseen door closed behind Him. The door was not seen by any of the newly arrived saints, nor was there any semblance of an opening in their new temporary home. All around them was just indescribable beauty— more than we could possibly imagine in our mortal form. Everything was new and exciting to them.

As wonderful as it all was, it was just a foretaste of what was soon to be given to them, and to be given to all who will believe in the atoning work of Yeshua, God's Son. That is why angels were assigned to minister to them, to prepare them for their forthcoming journey to Heaven with Yeshua. An unspeakable joy did abound there among the saints and much praise was freely given to God and to Yeshua.

With captivity freed and waiting in Paradise, Yeshua started down the long corridor to His next assignment. And for the first time since His Father had turned His face away from Him, He heard the voice He so loved, and so longed to hear, "You have done well, My Son. Your death has purchased all of the sins of every generation, past, present and future. Your blood has been a fair settlement for the remission of all sin. Yet there is still one more thing You must do for the work of redemption to be complete."

"Yes, My Father," came His reply. "I eagerly anticipate this last task." The Father proceeded to tell Him to go back to the tomb in which His earthly body lay. There, on the soon to be morning of the first day of the week, God would do His greatest miracle.

God, through Yeshua, during His ministry on earth, had raised numerous souls from death. Yet as miraculous as these were, they fell short of what was to happen in just a few short earth hours.

In the time it took for Yeshua to traverse back to the tomb, His Father's comforting voice, with angels' accompaniment refreshed the spirit of the Son of God.

"Father," Yeshua said, "it is good to hear Your voice again. It was the most difficult thing I have ever had to do, to see You turn Your back to Me, and to not be in fellowship with You. The pain of separation from You and the torment of the lost souls in Hades hurt more than the scourging at the pillar, the crown made of thorns, or the nails driven into my hands and feet. The separation had hurt more than the humiliation from the people." Then He asked with deep emotion, "If I could not bear it, how will mankind be able to?"

"My Son," His Father replied, "If they knew Me the way You know Me, they could not. They live their lives in ignorance of Me. They have many earthly pains and hurts, sorrows and grievings. Yet as they have rejected all whom I have sent to this point, and if they reject the work You have done, as those still in Hades did, they shall know for all eternity the pain and torment that comes with separation from Me. It is not the way I would have it to be. I would have it that all mankind would come to Me for all their needs. That is why I have sent You. That is why I have given You the twelve. The words they speak and write for every following generation will be to show the way to My forgiveness. Even still, many will reject You and Your teachings as the one did. Deception will grow stronger in the earth.

Yet You shall have disciples in every generation. Their job shall be to reveal You to their fellow man. Also, as You have made me known to Your followers, they shall make me known also. We shall work many miracles through them, and many shall be saved because of their witness. It shall be so only if those who choose to follow You are faithful to do the work that You died to make possible."

The Father also said to His Son, "It is not My desire that any should perish from My presence. Your followers must be filled with My Spirit, walking in My power and in the fruit of My Spirit. They must be willing to leave all for Your sake. They must love the lost even as You love them, willing even to lay down their lives for them. As the ages pass and the end of the age approaches, it shall continually grow harder and harder for them to penetrate the darkness. Each generation will bring greater deception. That is why You must fulfill this last act. To give to all who choose to follow You a greater hope than they now see for themselves."

Yeshua's Father continued to speak to Him, "You must now return to Your earthly shell and spend a short time with the eleven. They must all know that death is not the final act of life—that there is a resurrection from death at the end of the age. That is to be their encouragement, and their motivation. Not that their sins are forgiven only, but that by believing they shall also live and reign with You forever, in a world where it will be like it was always supposed to be."

"Father," Yeshua said, "You have made the heart of My spirit rejoice. I shall be most happy to glorify You in the earth. I shall greatly rejoice in revealing Your great power and love for what time I have left before our joyous reunion."

God gave His Son final instructions before the glorious moment arrived. "Son, let no person touch You, after You are risen from death, until You have come to see Me. You shall be revealed to a few, but no one is to touch You."

"I understand My Father," Yeshua said as he stood in the cold, dark tomb that housed His earthly body. "I understand, and I will honor Your command."

15
The Resurrection

As Yeshua stood there in the cold
blackness,

He was for an instant reminded of the
cold, black reality of death;

The torment He had witnessed in Hades
of the souls left behind forever;

The torment of their spending eternity
without God.

He remembered what His Father had
just told Him concerning the fate of those still
living and those yet to live who would reject
His sacrifice for their sins.

It must not happen, He thought.

Still, in His great heart He knew that
not everyone would believe in Him, that
they would choose rather to believe the lie
perpetrated by the adversary, Satan.

As suddenly as the afternoon sky had
turned as dark as night three days ago on the
hill called Golgotha, a radiant light began to
fill the cold, damp darkness of the tomb. The
light kept growing brighter as the minutes
passed by. It was during the onslaught of the
radiant light that Yeshua's spirit and soul were
reunited with His earthly body.

Outside the tomb the four Roman soldiers keeping watch, shivered around a fire in the cold of the early morning. "I'll be glad when this watch is over," one of them said. "Who's stupid idea was this anyway, placing a guard around the tomb of a dead man?"

"It does not make any sense to me either," spoke up another as he rubbed his hands together over the slowly dying flame.

The third soldier, the youngest of the four then said, "The High Priest is afraid some of His followers are going to steal the body and hide it, and claim that the dead man is alive, or something like that."

"Superstitious lot, all of them," the first soldier added.

"Just a couple of more hours and we can get back to our normal lives," spoke the commander of the guard. "Besides, none of the others that I have talked with have seen or heard anything of this man's followers since the day He was buried. They will not come. Wait and see. Life will return to normal." With those words the soldiers waited silently, shivering against the dawn.

Behind the stone-sealed entrance of the tomb, basking in Heavenly radiance, Yeshua stood with two of His Father's faithful angels. The radiant light, the glory of God, left no shadow of darkness as it engulfed Yeshua and His two ministering companions. Yeshua drank in His Father's glory like a man deprived of water in the heat of the desert sun.

The brilliant radiant light that now saturated every inch of the tomb was seen once before in man's history on earth.

Thirty-three years ago it appeared as a bright star in the Bethlehem sky.

The star that shone on the night Yeshua was born.

The same star that had led the Wisemen from the east with their prophetic gifts to present to the new-born king.

Now that same great light was building up in the tomb,
Ready to shine upon the earth once again.

Two of the guards lay nearly asleep on the ground, while two stayed awake and talked. They were not in guard posture but they were professional soldiers always at the ready. The stillness of the morning air was suddenly disturbed by a wind that came out of nowhere, waking the two drowsing soldiers. In a frenzy, the four soldiers hurried to form a wall against the wind with their shields. If they had been fully alert, they would have noticed that trees only a hundred feet away were perfectly still. In their confusion they had missed that. All they were concerned with was keeping the fire burning. As frantically as they tried to shield the fire, the wind won out. They were cold before the wind came, now they were colder and not very happy with this added inconvenience. But they dared not leave their post until their watch was up.

One of the angels with Yeshua spoke, "It is time." With those words they both disappeared through the wall of the tomb. Outside, and still invisible, they readied themselves.

"Peace, soldiers," they both spoke in unison after taking on human form.

"What? Who goes there?" spoke the startled commander. As he drew his sword to strike one of the intruders, the ground suddenly began to quake violently under them. In shock, the four soldiers could only stare at the scene unfolding before them.

The two angels stood about ten feet from the entrance to the tomb, hands lifted to Heaven, while a song of such beauty come forth from their lips. As the earth continued to shake, the seal around the stone began to fall off in pieces.

Rays of radiant light began to shine out through the resulting holes. The stunned soldiers, blinded by the brightness of the light and the sudden appearance of the two men, turned their faces away for a moment, trying to gather their composure, but, overcome with fear, they fainted and fell helplessly to the shaking ground, as dead men.

A moment later, the large stone that had sealed the tomb was rolled off to one side. The cold early morning air was now being warmed by the light coming from the tomb. The angels on the ground, and those in Heaven were on their knees as they observed the spectacle now taking place before their eyes. The scene they had been waiting millennia to witness.

Inside the now opened tomb, the triumphant Yeshua stood bathed in the light of the glory of God.

"Go forth Son," the voice of His Father was heard saying above the sound of the mighty wind outside the cave.

Triumphantly, Yeshua, the Son of God, stepped through the tomb opening. At that moment, death passed into life.

The kneeling angels were now prostrate before their King, the risen Savior of mankind.

In the Heavens, choruses of angelic praise were being sung with more jubilation than at any time in the history of creation.

The saints in Paradise, able also to watch the marvelous scene unfolding on earth, joined in the chorus of praise to God.

In Hades, fear and trembling were multiplied with the knowledge of the resurrection from the dead of the Son of God. What the adversary thought he had won, was now lost forever.

16

Yeshua

Yeshua,
The only begotten Son
Of the only true God,
Has risen from the grave.

He has conquered death.
He has defeated
The enemy of our souls,
The deceiver, Satan.
He has fulfilled
The plan of God
For our redemption.

The plan to redeem fallen man from
the curse of death and separation from God,
handed down to all generations from Adam,
was carried out those three days and nights.
God had purposed His Son, Yeshua, to die
for the sins of fallen mankind. Yeshua, in
loving obedience, had fulfilled the Father's
plan. Mankind could once again have
fellowship with God through Yeshua.

יֵשׁוּעַ הַמָּשִׁיחַ

Not by their good works or intentions,
But by the blood of God's own Son,

YESHUA, HA MASHIACH
 (JESUS THE MESSIAH).

KING OF KINGS
 AND
LORD OF LORDS.

THANK YOU, YESHUA.

HE IS ALIVE!

17
The Cry

This cry has reverberated
Through the corridors of time
For almost twenty centuries.
Yeshua was alive then,
The day God raised Him from death.
He is still alive today.
He was victorious then.
Today, through Him,
We are victorious also.
He died to forgive sin then.
We still can find forgiveness today,
Two thousand years later.
All we have to do is ask for it.
If we confess our sins,
He (God) is faithful and just
To forgive us our sins, and
To cleanse us from all unrighteousness
     (1 John 1:9).

For God so loved the world
That He gave His only begotten Son,
That whoever believes in Him
Should not perish
But have everlasting life (John 3:16).

God gave His Son Yeshua for us.
Yeshua gave His life for our sins.

All that is required of us is to believe
this truth and receive the free gift of salvation
offered to us in Yeshua.

But as many as received Him (Yeshua),
To them He gave the right (authority)
To become children of God,
To those who believe in His name
    (John 1:12).

To all who make the choice to receive
    Yeshua,
There is no end to this story.
As He lives on, even today,
So shall we also live on eternally with
    Him.
To all who choose not to believe in and
    receive Him . . .

THE END

This book is available at:

olivepresspublisher.com

amazon.com

barnesandnoble.com

and other websites.

The E-book is available at:

amazon.com

Book stores and distributors
may obtain this book
at 40% discount through:
Ingram Book Company
or
Olive Press Publisher:
olivepressbooks@gmail.com

www.ingramcontent.com/pod-product-compliance
Lightning Source LLC
Chambersburg PA
CBHW071102040426
42443CB00013B/3375